Pebble® Plus

Creepy Crawlers

Cockroaches

by Lisa J. Amstutz

Gail Saunders-Smith, PhD, Consulting Editor

Consultant: Wade Harrell
Vice President
American Tarantula Society

CAPSTONE PRESS
a capstone imprint

Pebble Plus is published by Capstone Press,
1710 Roe Crest Drive, North Mankato, Minnesota 56003.
www.capstonepub.com

Library of Congress Cataloging-in-Publication Data
Amstutz, Lisa J.
Cockroaches / by Lisa J. Amstutz.
p. cm.—(Pebble Plus. Creepy Crawlers)
Summary: "Learn about cockroaches, including how and where they live
and how these creepy creatures are important parts of their world"—Provided by publisher.
Audience: 005-008.
Audience: K to grade 3.
Includes bibliographical references and index.
ISBN 978-1-4765-2063-6 (library binding)
ISBN 978-1-4296-3478-7 (eBook PDF)
1. Cockroaches—Juvenile literature. I. Title.
QL505.5.A47 2014
595.7'28—dc23   2013008523

Editorial Credits
Jeni Wittrock, editor; Kyle Grenz, designer; Laura Manthe, production specialist

Photo Credits
Alamy: blickwinkel, 19, Clownfishphoto, 13, Nigel Cattlin, 9, Premaphotos, 7, 17; National Geographic Stock: Bates Littlehales, 5, Darlyne A. Murawski, 15; Science Source: James H. Robinson, 11; Shutterstock: formiktopus, 21, Grauvision, cover, Mau Horng, 1, vlastas66, design element (throughout)

Note to Parents and Teachers

The Creepy Crawlers set supports national science standards related to life science. This book describes and illustrates cockroaches. The images support early readers in understanding the text. The repetition of words and phrases helps early readers learn new words. This book also introduces early readers to subject-specific vocabulary words, which are defined in the Glossary section. Early readers may need assistance to read some words and to use the Table of Contents, Glossary, Read More, Internet Sites, and Index sections of the book.

Printed in China by Nordica.
0413/CA21300494
032013   007226NORDF13

Table of Contents

A Need for Speed

Hurry-scurry!

A cockroach is one of

the world's fastest insects.

Some cockroaches run about

50 body lengths per second!

Cockroaches are often found in warm, damp places. They live in North and South America, Asia, Europe, and Australia. Their colors match tree bark and soil.

A few kinds of cockroaches are pests. They live where people live and work. They can spread germs. Most roaches are not found near people.

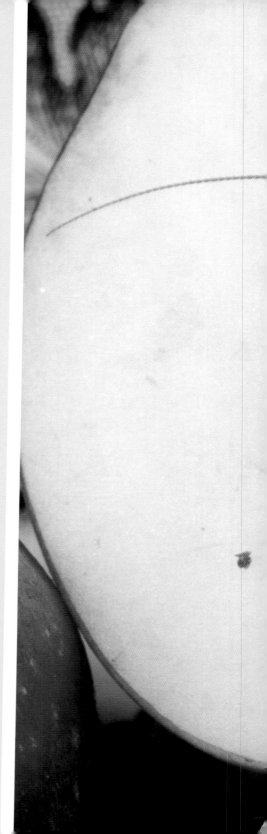

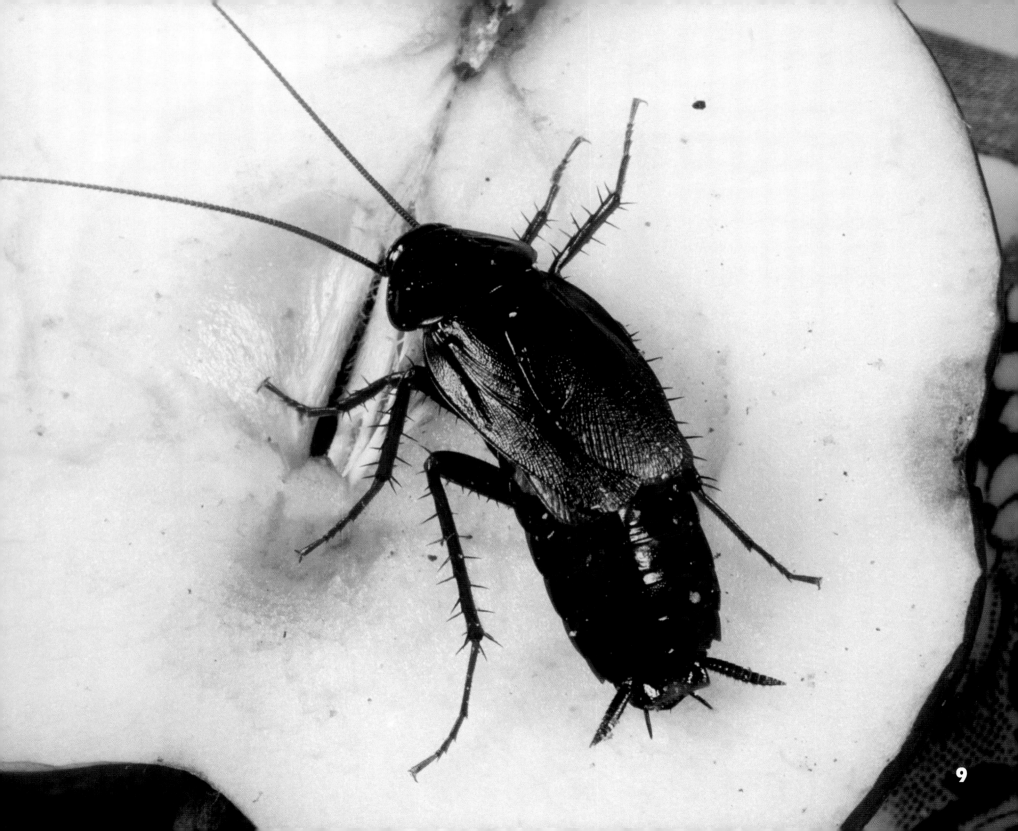

9

Cockroach Bodies

Cockroaches have small, flat bodies. Six bent legs with claws help them run and climb. Most adult roaches have wings, but they are not good fliers.

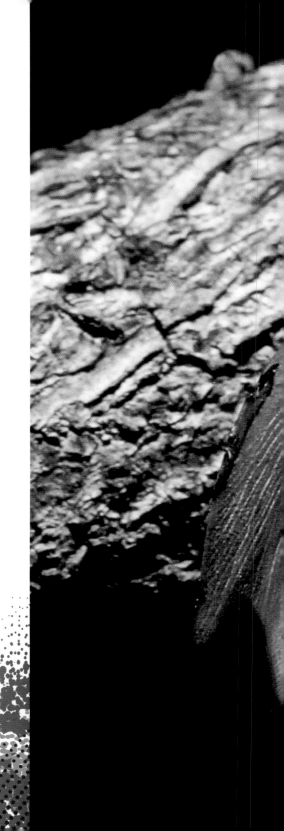

Roaches do not see well.
Feelers and antennae
sense where they are going
and what is around them.

feeler

antenna

Finding Food

Cockroaches come out to eat when it's dark. Their good sense of smell helps them find food. Roaches taste food with mouth parts called palpi.

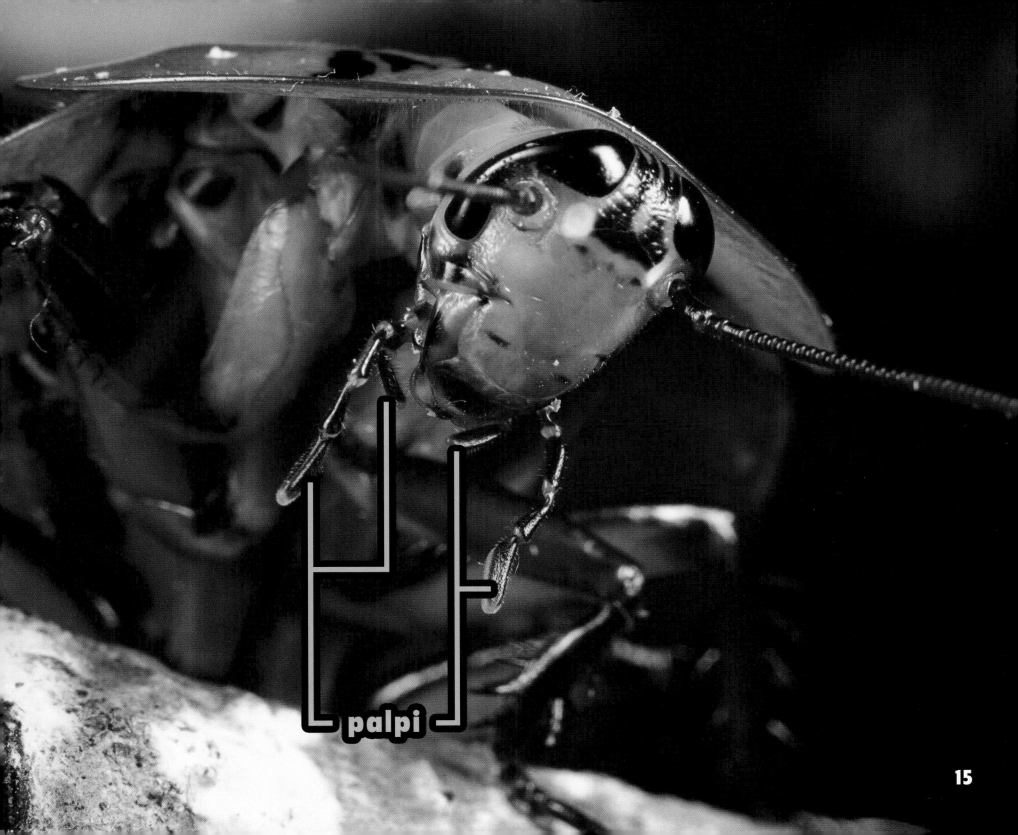

palpi

Chomp! Cockroaches chew
food with their strong jaws.
Roaches are scavengers.
They will eat almost anything,
even soap and glue!

A Roach's Life

Most female cockroaches make egg cases. Young nymphs hatch from the egg case. Roaches molt, or shed their skins, as they grow.

egg case

19

Birds, lizards, spiders, rats, and other animals eat roaches. But cockroaches are fast and sneaky. A roach's creepy body helps it stay safe.

Glossary

antenna—a feeler on an animal's head

claw—a hard, curved nail on the foot of an animal

damp—slightly wet

germ—a very small living organism that can
cause disease

insect—aa small animal with a hard outer shell, six legs,
three body sections, and two antennae

nymph—a young form of an insect; nymphs change
into adults by shedding their skin many times

palpus—one of two small feelers, or palpi, on an insect's
mouth that holds and tastes food

pest—an animal that is harmful or bothersome
to humans

scavenger—an animal that feeds on whatever it can find

sense—to feel

Read More

Bodden, Valerie. *Cockroaches.* Creepy Creatures. Mankato, Minn.: Creative Education: 2013.

Helget, Nichole. *Cockroaches.* Mankato, Minn.: Creative Education, 2008.

Roza, Greg. *Repulsive Cockroaches.* World of Bugs. New York: Gareth Stevens Pub., 2011.

Internet Sites

FactHound offers a safe, fun way to find Internet sites related to this book. All of the sites on FactHound have been researched by our staff.

Here's all you do:

Visit *www.facthound.com*

Type in this code: 9781476520636

Super-cool stuff! Check out projects, games and lots more at
www.capstonekids.com

Index

Word Count: 205
Grade: 1
Early-Intervention Level: 18